TITANIC

FRANKLIN WATTS
NEW YORK / LONDON / TORONTO / SYDNEY   1987 / A FIRST BOOK

FRANK SLOAN

TITANIC

The author is particularly grateful to
Frank O. Braynard, Richard Chandler of
Woods Hole Oceanographic Institution,
and Ken Marschall, who offered valuable
criticisms of the manuscript.

Thanks to Ken Benson, Michael Cooper, and
Marjory Kline, all of whom turned up with
Titanic memorabilia and material.

I am also especially indebted to Cass R. Sandak,
whose suggestions and ideas were invaluable.

F.S.

Original painting by Ken Marschall;
from the collection of Dennis R. Kromm
Cover design by Honi Werner

Photographs courtesy of: The Bettmann
Archive, Inc.: pp. 2–3, 43, 46, 53, 59;
Philadelphia Maritime Museum: pp. 13,
28; Brown Brothers: pp. 18, 26, 33,
50, 54; Harland & Wolff: pp. 25, 29;
Popperfoto: p. 35; Culver Pictures, Inc.: p. 52;
Movie Star News: p. 66; Woods Hole Ocean-
ographic Institution: pp. 73, 78, 80, 81.

Library of Congress Cataloging-in-Publication Data

Sloan, Frank.
Titanic.

(A First book)
Bibliography: p.
Includes index.
Summary: Describes the ocean liner Titanic, its
maiden voyage, and its sinking, and discusses the
recent discovery and exploration of the ship's
remains on the ocean floor using deep-diving robots.
1. Titanic (Steamship)—Juvenile literature.
2. Shipwrecks—North Atlantic Ocean—Juvenile
literature. [1. Titanic (Steamship) 2. Shipwrecks]
I. Title.
G530.T6S58   1987   363.1′23′091631   87-6214
ISBN 0-531-10396-X

CONTENTS

TITANIC

from
The Convergence of the Twain

. . . And as the smart ship grew,
In stature, grace and hue,
In shadowy silent distance grew the iceberg too.

Alien they seemed to be
No mortal eye could see
The intimate welding of their later history.

Thomas Hardy

CHAPTER ONE

A MILLION
TO ONE

On September 1, 1985, one of the most intriguing mysteries of the twentieth century was solved. For almost seventy-five years, the world had wanted to know *exactly* what had happened to the *Titanic*, the giant liner that struck an iceberg and sank shortly after while she was on her maiden voyage to New York in 1912. For all that time, adventurers had wondered precisely where the ship was and what kind of shape the wreck was in. Would the wreck, once found, yield up untold treasures? Were there still bodies on the ocean bottom, preserved in the dark waters? What would the years of silence disclose?

This is the story of that ill-fated voyage and what has been learned since 1985.

Shortly before midnight on Sunday, April 14, 1912, the largest liner in the world struck an iceberg in the North Atlantic. A little more than two and half hours later, Britain's R.M.S. *Titanic* sank, and around 1,500 people lost their lives. The *Titanic*'s sinking was the worst maritime disaster ever to take place during peacetime, and it was one of the most incredible accidents that could have occurred. Many people had described the liner as "unsinkable." No one believed that *anything* could cause the *Titanic* to sink. And no one could foresee that it would happen on the grand ship's maiden voyage, or first Atlantic crossing. The odds against the *Titanic* going down were probably a million to one.

The event took place more than seventy-five years ago. The world was different then. The twentieth century was just twelve years old. The British Empire was at its height, and America had emerged from the nineteenth century as a power to equal any in the world. Radio and television didn't exist. Women had not yet been given the right to vote. The automobile was still a rare and luxurious item. World Wars I and II hadn't been fought. There was innocence and confidence. And people, including many immigrants who had just arrived in America, were full of hope for the future. But at the same time there was also widespread political unrest, poverty, and unhappiness.

The impact of the *Titanic*'s last hours was enormous. The deaths of so many people were of great interest to the general public. Many of the passengers on the ship were wealthy and some were famous. They were like the rock and movie stars and sports celebrities of today. In 1912 the liner represented the last word in technology and progress. The public's response to the sinking must have been similar to the way we felt after the space shuttle *Challenger* was destroyed in 1986. It simply couldn't happen. But it did.

Steamships had been crossing the Atlantic on a regular basis since the 1840s, and many well-known and popular liners carried people back and forth. The rich traveled on fast ships,

*Onlookers wave bon voyage as the
great ship begins its fatal journey.*

tasteful floating hotels that re-created the most luxurious and glamorous hotels and public buildings on land. In the days when ocean travel was popular, ships almost took on personalities, and many people would seek out the same ship over and over again, much the way people today like to stay at the same hotel—sometimes in the same room—over and over again.

Wealthy passengers traveled on the upper decks of ships. They had luxurious staterooms and elegantly decorated public rooms where they could amuse themselves during the voyage, which could last from five to fourteen days.

But the poor traveled in third class in the bottom and the back of the boat, where the noise and motion were most noticeable. This part of the ship was called steerage, and the quarters were often filthy and cramped. It was known as steerage because cattle had once been carried on the trip from America to Europe. And immigrants were herded in like cattle on the return voyage. Most of these people were on their way to the land of opportunity, to build new lives in America, and getting there made any conditions they had to endure worth it.

WHERE DOES
THE STORY BEGIN?

Where and when does the story of the *Titanic* really begin?

Does it begin in the late nineteenth century? In those days there were neither jets nor propeller-driven airplanes that could cross the Atlantic in a few hours. There was a need for large ships to carry travelers between America and Europe. And ships were the only way to go. Bigger and bigger ships were needed all the time to transport the people from Europe who wanted to emigrate and settle in America.

Or does the story begin in 1902? That is the year when the American financier J.P. Morgan and other investors formed a group called the International Mercantile Marine. This company would eventually purchase the White Star Line, the *Titanic*'s owners, for $25 million in gold.

Or does it begin in 1907, the year that saw over 1,200,000 immigrants arrive in the United States? There was competition among the steamship lines to carry the most people. They all knew there was a great deal of money to be made from the immigrant traffic. And the steamship lines needed ships to carry these immigrants.

In that same year, the Cunard Line introduced its two large luxury liners, the *Mauretania* and the *Lusitania*. In just a short while these ships became the most popular for crossing the Atlantic. They were popular because they were the fastest ships afloat. The White Star Line, Cunard's great rival for transatlantic passengers, had no ships as big or as fast. It wanted to outstrip Cunard's popular ships with luxury liners of its own. So the owners of the White Star Line began to dream. And the company's designers and naval architects began to plan for the future.

Perhaps the story begins when two momentous things happened on the same day. On May 31, 1911, the *Olympic,* the White Star Line's brand-new flagship, began her maiden voyage from England to America. At almost the same time of day, the *Olympic*'s slightly larger sister ship, the *Titanic,* was launched at the Harland & Wolff shipyards in Belfast, Northern Ireland. Neither ship would be faster than the *Mauretania* and the *Lusitania,* but each was larger. And they would be the most luxurious ships afloat.

When the *Titanic* was launched, the ship was far from complete. During the next ten months, the great ship was fitted out. This means that the masts and funnels were added. The interior electrical equipment and boilers that ran the ship were also installed. And the final touches were put on the sumptuous interior decorations.

Or does the story of the *Titanic* begin as the great liner left Great Britain on its maiden voyage? The ship steamed majestically away from the dock in Southampton, bound for Cherbourg, France. There she would pick up additional passengers and then head for Queenstown, Ireland. At Queenstown the ship would make a last stop and pick up further passengers for the seven-day voyage to New York.

The date was Wednesday, April 10, 1912.

CHAPTER TWO

THE GREAT
SHIP SAILS

The maiden voyage of the *Titanic* began uneventfully enough at noon on that April 10. Because of a coal strike in Great Britain, there was confusion about when the new liner was going to sail. The *Titanic* needed an unheard-of 650 tons of coal a day to keep her boilers at full steam. To save coal, other ships had canceled their sailings. The *Titanic*'s passenger list was not full. In fact, she was filled to only about 60 percent of her passenger capacity.

As the ship left her Southampton dock, everything seemed to be working beautifully. But then something unexpected—and almost unfortunate—happened. As the *Titanic* passed two other vessels moored side by side at their pier, the suction from the *Titanic* pulled one of the vessels loose. The *New York* pulled away from the *Oceanic* and narrowly missed crashing into the side of the departing *Titanic* by just a few feet.

Captain E.J. Smith of the *Titanic* used his head and quickly ordered a round turn and stopped the *Titanic*'s engines. As her propellers stopped, so did the suction. This got the *Titanic* out of

The Titanic *narrowly escapes collision as*
she leaves Southampton on April 10, 1912.
The suction of her propellers tore the
American liner New York *from her moorings.*

the other ship's path, and the new liner was on her way. Disaster had been narrowly averted.

To many on board, including the crew, it seemed an ominous beginning. And in years to come this small incident would take on significance as an example of the *Titanic*'s "bad luck." Even before that accident, twenty-two men who had signed on as crew members disappeared and never showed up. There were whispers that she was an unlucky ship.

Some people even said the *Titanic* was jinxed because she had a mummy in the hold, a mummy that carried a curse with it. Others spoke in hushed tones of a great Buddha with an evil spell. Hidden in Captain Smith's safe, it too was supposed to carry bad luck with it.

VITAL STATISTICS

A ship's maiden voyage always caused great excitement. And because the *Titanic* was the world's largest ship, this was a particularly momentous occasion. She was known as R.M.S. *Titanic*, for Royal Mail Ship. Indeed, on her first and only trip, the *Titanic* carried almost 3,500 bags of mail in addition to 900 tons of baggage.

The *Titanic* measured 46,328 gross tons, which made her 50 percent larger than any other boat afloat. Gross tonnage is the most common manner of "weighing" a ship. It is actually a cubic measurement of size. And "she" and "her" are the traditional nautical pronouns used to refer to a ship.

The *Titanic* was 883 feet (260 m) long from front to back. This is about the same as four city blocks. The ship was 92.5 feet (30 m) wide in the middle, the widest part. From her keel, or bottom, to

INQUIRY INTO THE LOSS OF THE "TITANIC"; LONGITUDINAL SECTION AND PLANS SHOWING BULKHEADS, MEANS OF EGRESS FROM LOWER DECKS

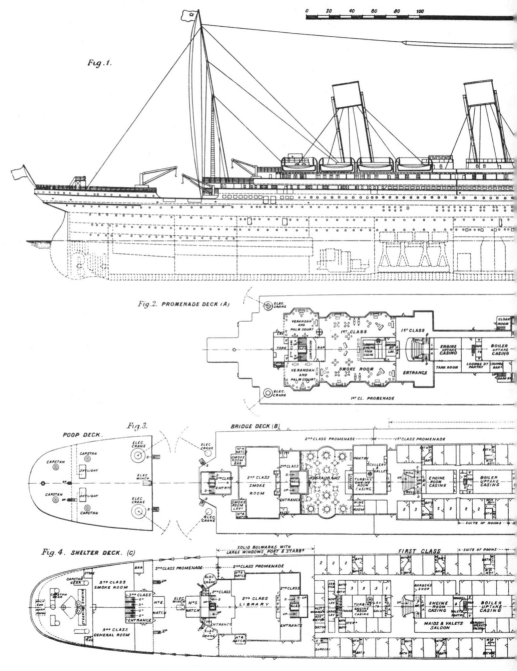

Fig.1.

Fig.2. PROMENADE DECK (A)

Fig.3.

POOP DECK.

BRIDGE DECK (B)

Fig.4. SHELTER DECK. (C)

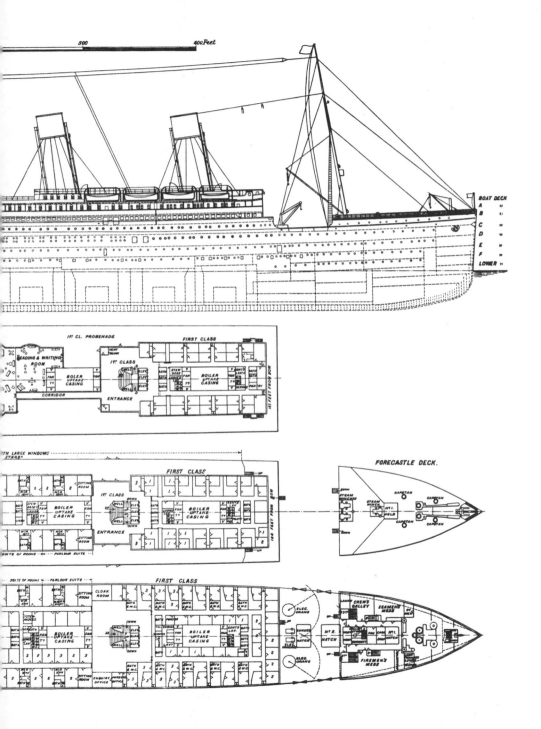

INQUIRY INTO THE LOSS OF THE "TITANIC"; PLANS SHOWING BULKHEADS, MEANS OF EGRESS FROM LOWER DECKS

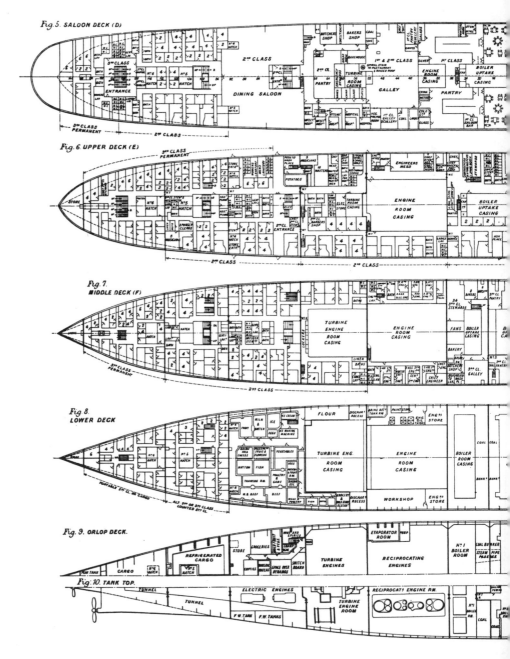

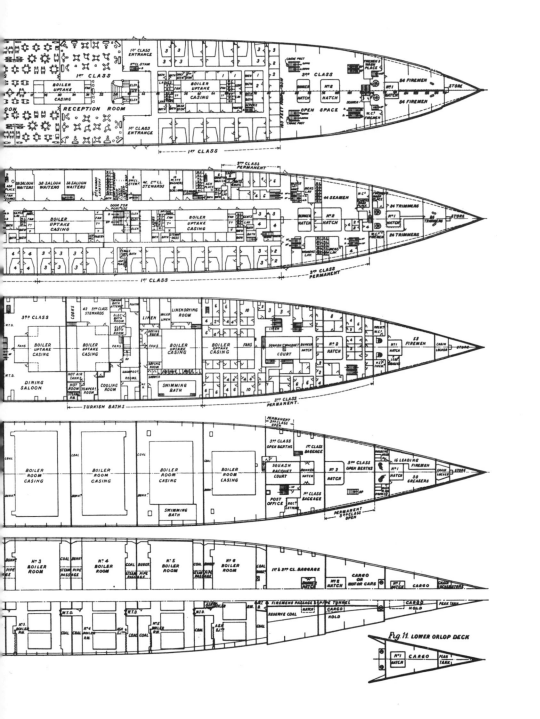

Fig. 11. LOWER ORLOP DECK

the top of the bridge (the highest part of the superstructure) she measured 104 feet (30 m), almost as high as an eleven-story building. She cost over $10 million in 1912 money to build.

The *Titanic* had four majestic smokestacks, or funnels. In the heyday of great ships a four-stacked liner was a symbol of elegance and luxury. Three of the funnels were actually used for carrying off smoke and steam, but the fourth was a dummy and was used as a ventilator. Each smokestack averaged 62 feet (19 m) high and was 22 feet (6.5 m) across. Two train locomotives, side by side, could fit in each funnel.

Because she had a double bottom the great liner was heralded as "unsinkable." This meant that the hull was constructed with two coats of steel, one inside the other. But there was a flaw: the double coating did not extend very far up the sides of the ship. She also had sixteen watertight compartments. Even if, by some extraordinary circumstance, as many as two of these compartments were to fill with water, the ship could still remain afloat.

The *Titanic*'s sister ship, the *Olympic,* had been in service for almost a year and in that short time had become popular with North Atlantic travelers. But the *Titanic* had a few features the *Olympic* didn't have. The front end of the promenade deck on the *Titanic* was glassed in. This was almost a necessity for sheltering passengers on the often frigid crossing. The *Titanic* also sported

This was just one of the styles of furnishings in the first-class cabins.

*First-class passengers could enjoy dining
in a Parisian café on B deck.*

a set of staterooms on B deck that had real windows, not port-holes. The *Titanic* offered a café on B deck that was designed to give passengers the feeling of dining at one of the sidewalk cafés of Paris.

The ship was divided into three classes: first, second, and third. Most of the space on the ship, especially in the middle of the ship and on the upper decks, was given over to first class. Second class was the smallest and had simple but tasteful public rooms on upper decks, toward the rear of the ship. Third class (steerage) passengers were given modest space furthest down in the boat. Although steerage on the *Titanic* was plain, it was clean, which it emphatically wasn't on some of the Atlantic ships. Single men in third class were segregated from the women— each at opposite ends of the ship. Families were allowed to berth together. On this crossing, as on most voyages to the United States, many of the immigrants had come from all parts of Europe and spoke little or no English.

Third-class passengers had very little deck space and their public rooms were small but comfortable. Gates were set up be-tween the accommodations to keep the classes from mingling. It was strictly forbidden to go from second or third classes into first, although it was a traditional shipboard "game" to try to do so.

GETTING USED TO THE SHIP

The passengers spent most of the first day settling in and making themselves comfortable for the voyage. They were getting used to the ship and getting to know as many of its luxurious features as possible. After all, this was a ship whose fittings equaled those of the most elegant buildings on shore. The spacious public rooms

*The second-class promenade on the
port side of the boat deck*

*The grand staircase in first class was covered
by an ornate dome of leaded glass.*

were parlors furnished with deep carpets, pianos, easy chairs, and great sofas.

Shortly after the ship got under way, deck stewards were busy setting up deck chairs in the open space. Not long after that pots of steaming tea and small sandwiches and cakes would be passed around. Active people could work out in the gymnasium or indulge in games of shuffleboard or quoits on spacious outdoor decks reserved for first-class passengers.

Most of the passengers in first class were wealthy Americans, including heirs to some of the greatest fortunes. The *Titanic* and the *Olympic* had been built with Americans in mind, while the *Lusitania* and the *Mauretania* were extremely popular with British travelers. The passenger list contained people with a total wealth of more than a quarter of a billion dollars. Many of the wealthiest first-class passengers had maids or valets to unpack the great numbers of trunks and suitcases that would be needed during the trip.

Not only were the passengers getting used to the ship—as they had to on every voyage—but so were the crew members. Because the *Titanic* was a new and important ship, the crew had been picked very carefully. The White Star Line had spared no expense in staffing the *Titanic*. Of the 900 crew members, about 500 were like hotel staff. They were stewards and maids who worked above decks, constantly on duty, seeing to the passengers' needs. And after passengers went to sleep at night, cleaners readied the ship for the next day. Chefs, waiters, and busboys all staffed the various kitchens and dining rooms. There were nine "bootblacks" whose only job was to be sure that passengers' shoes were polished. Two small orchestras, one made up of five musicians and another of three, played soft background melodies.

Far down, at the bottom of the ship, were the "greasers," the engineers and stokers. These were the men who shoveled coal into the ship's great furnaces to keep her steaming at such a fast speed. And everywhere else, throughout the ship, were the officers. These men, ranking just under the captain, were responsible for supervising the rest of the crew. They all worked together to make sure the ship was running smoothly.

Two of the crew members whose names would become well known a short time later were busy in the wireless room. Also known as the Marconi station, this small room at the top of the ship was staffed by John G. Phillips and Harold Bride. Their biggest job was to receive radiograms, also known as radiotelegrams or marconigrams, which told passengers what was happening back on land. They also, of course, sent telegrams back to land. Radio telegraphic transmission was, in 1912, a fairly new science. No one dreamed that in a few days it would save many lives.

On the top decks, in sumptuous luxury, there were some very distinguished passengers: Colonel John Jacob Astor and his new wife; Isidor Straus, the department store owner, and his wife; the Philadelphia financier George Widener; President Taft's military aide, Major Archibald Butt; and the financier Benjamin Guggenheim.

Other important first-class passengers included Jacques Futrelle, a writer and a contributor to the *Saturday Evening Post*; theater manager Henry B. Harris; the popular artist Francis David Millet; William T. Stead, a spiritualist and an editor; and the engineer Washington Augustus Roebling, who had been responsible for building the Brooklyn Bridge.

One of the other prominent passengers was Bruce Ismay, the managing director of the White Star Line and one of the few men to survive the sinking of the *Titanic*. As the most distinguished representative of the White Star Line on board, he had good reason to be proud of the new ship. Although the *Titanic* wasn't due in New York until the following Wednesday morning, there was some feeling that Ismay would urge Captain Smith to speed the vessel in order to arrive late Tuesday evening.

LUXURY AT SEA

First-class passengers paid $4,350, or about $50,000 in today's money, to stay in one of the *Titanic*'s elegant suites. The cost of passage included meals in the dining rooms. Only drinks and specially ordered food were extra. The one-way fare for second-class passengers was $65 and up. Steerage passengers paid an average of only $35 for the chance to cross the Atlantic.

The first-class public rooms were spacious and elegantly fitted out with mirrors, crystal light fixtures, and potted plants. There was a great lounge and a smoking room, usually reserved for male travelers. An enormous dining room (or dining saloon, as it was called in those days) was on D deck. It was as wide as the ship itself and could seat over 500 people at one time. In addition, the ship featured a restaurant, where very special and private meals could be served—at considerable additional cost. The kitchens on board were among the best equipped and most modern to be found anywhere.

The Turkish bath had a red ceiling
crisscrossed with gilded beams and
supported by columns encased in teakwood.
Blue-green tiles decorated the walls.

The *Titanic*'s four elevators had richly carved wooden paneling; the palm court featured an elaborate trellis with plants twined around it; and there was even a Turkish bath. Pets were kept in a kennel where they could be visited by their concerned owners. A separate lounge was provided for the maids and valets of the wealthy passengers.

By evening on the first day, the *Titanic* had crossed the English Channel to France. The ship was too big to dock in Cherbourg. A smaller boat, called a tender, brought the new passengers to a spot just outside the harbor entrance where the *Titanic* was anchored. Within a few hours the passengers and their baggage had been loaded and the ship was under way once again.

The next morning, on Thursday the eleventh of April, the ship was approaching Queenstown, Ireland. There she would make a last stop before heading out into the Atlantic and crossing to New York. By 1:30 P.M. the *Titanic* had loaded her final passengers and was under way.

To the best of anyone's knowledge there were 1,316 passengers and 892 crew members on board, for a total of 2,208 people.

Captain Smith looks down from the starboard bridge wing while the ship is anchored at Queenstown, Ireland. One of the sixteen wooden lifeboats can be seen suspended from its davits.

Because the exact records went down with the ship, a completely accurate count will never be known. There may have been some passengers without tickets and some people who made last-minute changes. There may even have been a stowaway or two. Most sources report a total between 2,201 and 2,224 people on the *Titanic.*

By the morning of the twelfth the *Titanic* was well out in the Atlantic and sailing along at a speed of 21 knots. Knots are used to measure the speed of boats. One knot is 1 nautical mile per hour. A nautical mile is the same as 6,076 feet (1,852 m). It is slightly more than a mile on land. Although it does not sound like a very fast speed to us today, 21 knots made the *Titanic* a very speedy ship in 1912. And even today the speediest liners do not travel much faster.

The weather was fine, and the food and company were excellent. Passengers pronounced the ship a great success. The seas were calm and there were almost no cases of seasickness. And the ship herself performed well. There were very few complaints about vibration caused by the ship's engines or about rolling, two things that often made passengers uncomfortable.

Everyone had settled in, and the ship was becoming more like a luxurious home to most of the first-class passengers. A pattern was established of easy days followed by gourmet meals and evenings of dancing and card playing in the lavishly decorated public rooms. This routine was expected to continue until the ship arrived in New York, where she was due on Wednesday, April 17.

Passengers enjoyed the indoor swimming pool and the squash racket courts. Both of these were novelties on a ship and were very popular. A newspaper was published every morning on the *Titanic*. Specially prepared and printed on board the ship, it was called the *Atlantic Daily Bulletin*.

THE FATEFUL
SUNDAY EVENING

On Sunday evening the fourteenth, life was slightly quieter than usual. Religious services had been held earlier in the day. There had been a hymn sing in the dining room following dinner and, because it was a Sunday, dancing was not permitted. Card-playing would not normally have been allowed on an English ship on a Sunday, but perhaps because it was the ship's maiden voyage, some of the stricter rules had been relaxed.

The ship's speed had been increased slightly to 22.5 knots. The sea was calm, and during the course of the day, people had noticed that the weather was getting colder. By nightfall the temperature had dropped considerably, but the skies were clear and moonless.

Many of the passengers had gone to bed. Only a few die-hards were still up, having a last cigarette in the smoking room or playing a final hand of cards.

At 11:40 P.M. a few people on the upper decks noticed a slight jar. As described by one writer: "... the ship seemed to shake herself—just like a wet dog."

The nightmare had begun.

CHAPTER THREE

THE SHIP HITS
THE ICEBERG

Most of the passengers didn't even realize that anything serious had happened, let alone that the *Titanic* had just struck a floating mountain of ice. It had all happened in a matter of ten seconds. A few people rushed out on deck and saw pieces of ice on the decks. Some claimed they had seen an 80-foot-high (25 m) iceberg receding into the distance off the back of the starboard (right) side of the ship. For a long time, there was no concern: after all, the *Titanic* was unsinkable! Most first-class passengers slept on, and few realized that the next several hours were going to change their lives in all kinds of ways.

Who had spotted the iceberg? Two men were in a small bucketlike affair called the crow's nest that was fastened about halfway up the front mast. They were called lookouts, and their responsibility was to let the captain know as soon as possible if they saw any problems. They did see the berg, but not until it was too close to avoid the collision.

Most of the passengers were not aware that several times during the course of that Sunday, April 14, there had been warnings that the *Titanic* might come across ice in some form or other. There had been messages all day long from several other ships in the area. They stated that there was dangerous ice nearby. Although Captain Smith and his officers knew of the potential danger, most ot the messages were ignored.

Many of the passengers also didn't realize that when the boat struck the iceberg, some part of the ship below the waterline had been wrenched open. Water was rapidly filling the lower parts of the *Titanic*. For most of the last seventy-five years people had assumed that a 300-foot-long (90 m) gash had been ripped, as if by a can opener, along the lower part of the hull. Whatever the cause, the wound to the vessel was severe.

THE BEGINNING OF THE END

A deathwatch had begun. Captain Smith knew it, and so did many of his senior officers. As soon as the collision occurred, the captain ordered the ship to be stopped. This took nearly four minutes and the ship traveled almost half a mile (0.8 km) before she was fully stopped. Although alarms were immediately sounded and the doors between the watertight compartments shut, within ten minutes water had flooded the first three holds to depths of about 14 feet (4 m).

Captain Smith understood the severity of the accident. Smith was a distinguished veteran of thirty-eight years at sea. This was to have been his last voyage before he retired. Smith knew the ship was in trouble because he was an experienced sailor. He also knew because Thomas Andrews, the naval architect who had overseen the *Titanic*'s design, had told him. Andrews was on board and had been one of the first people to rush down to the bottom of the ship after the accident. There he had found water pouring in at a rate that was too fast for the pumps to carry it away. His training and instinct told him the ship could not survive.

The crew below deck were the next people to grasp the extent of the damage. They worked desperately to keep the water out. They managed to keep the electricity on board the ship running almost until the very end. They made the work of abandoning the ship safer and more orderly than it might otherwise have been. Since there was no need to keep the ship's engines running, every person turned to the task of pumping out the increasing flood of water. The engineers stayed below deck as long as possible.

Some other people who knew the severity of the accident were Harold Bride and John Phillips, the two wireless operators. Up in the wireless room they had been given instructions to begin sending distress calls.

By fifteen minutes after midnight on the fifteenth, the *Titanic* had sent out a distress call: "Have struck an iceberg. We are badly damaged. Lat. 41.46 N., long. 50.14 W." A second call, shortly after the first one, repeated the message, but also included the new SOS (save our ship) signal. There is some uncertainty about whether or not the *Titanic* was the first ship to use the signal. Some sources indicate that the *Arapahoe*, in trouble in 1909, had been the first. In any event, the *Titanic*, if not the very first ship, was one of the first ships to use the SOS signal.

The watertight compartments at the bottom of the ship's hull had begun to fill with water. Why? Simply because the compartment walls, or bulkheads, weren't high enough. The ship began—slowly at first—to sink from the bow, or front. As one

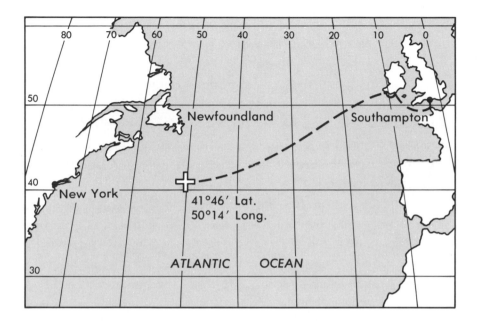

compartment began to overflow, the one next to it would then begin to fill up. And this pattern was repeated from the bow back to the stern, or tail, of the ship.

LEAVING THE SHIP

Most of the passengers still weren't aware that the ship was sinking. Many people had begun to assemble on deck in their life preservers. But they still felt there was no danger. After all, although it was very cold indeed, the sea was calm and there were even stars in the sky! But Captain Smith knew the worst. He knew the ship was doomed, and by 12:30, less than an hour after the collision, he had ordered all passengers to gather on the boat deck. Women and children would be helped into the lifeboats.

Even at this point, there was little panic. People began to sense that the great ship was in trouble, but they remained calm. Crew members were assigned to help people into lifeboats. But because the ship was new, many of the crew were not used to her. They weren't much surer than the passengers how to leave the ship. Due to the crew's uncertainty, many of the boats took a long time to lower.

Some of the boats were lowered half full, largely because many passengers weren't prepared to take the situation very seriously. As well, the crew was afraid that if the lifeboats were full, the added weight would cause these boats to crumple while they were suspended over the side. The crew was on a new ship and didn't realize that the lifeboats were among the few things that *had* been checked out carefully.

On a ship like the *Titanic,* the lifeboats were stored, covered by tarpaulins, on the top, or boat, deck. They were attached to upright metal poles, called davits, with a system of ropes and pulleys. Crew members would unfasten the boats and move them out over the sea. The boats would be lowered down one deck. Then passengers could, with great care, step into the boats. Finally the boats would be lowered further, all the way down to the sea. But the operation requires practice to be performed smoothly.

And that is what had been missing. There had not been any lifeboat drill on the earlier days of the voyage. A common practice on all ships, lifeboat drill was something Captain Smith appears to have been lax about. As a result, people didn't know

In the bygone era of the Titanic, one of the rules
of the sea was "women and children first" when a ship
had to be abandoned. This painting reflects the agony
of women bidding their husbands farewell, knowing
that they would probably never see them again.

which boats they had been assigned to or how to get to these boats quickly in an emergency.

Captain Smith was also aware of another fact: there weren't enough lifeboats for all the passengers. The ship had roughly 2,200 persons on board. A quick count of the fourteen 30-foot-long (9 m) lifeboats, two 25-foot-long (7.5 m) ones, and the four collapsible "Englehardt" lifeboats showed that their combined capacity, if fully loaded, was only 1,178. This meant that even if all the boats were loaded to their capacity, almost a thousand people could not be accommodated. They would have little chance of survival in the icy sea.

As they stood shivering on the tilting deck, the bewildered passengers began to realize that they *might* have to be inconvenienced and leave the ship. The calm was almost unearthly. Touching good-byes were said. Some of the men knew they were saying last farewells to their families. Some did not, and genuinely believed they would be reunited in just a few hours. Some women refused to be parted from their husbands and preferred to remain behind to face whatever might happen. Legend tells us that Mrs. Isidor Straus would not leave her husband, saying they had been together too long to be separated now. They then joined hands and sat side by side in deck chairs.

Passengers began to fill the lifeboats. Order prevailed as boat after boat, containing women and children and only partially filled, left the ship. Because the crew was inexperienced and poorly organized, the lifeboats could not all be lowered at the same time. Stories have come down of pistols being used to keep men out of the boats, of a man who dressed up as a woman in order to gain entrance to a boat, and of bribes being offered by wealthy people. But most accounts emphasize that there was little panic or confusion.

One of the wooden lifeboats to leave the *Titanic,* boat number 1, was lowered with only twelve people. It had been designed to hold forty. The four collapsible boats were awkwardly stored, very far away from the edge of the ship. They had to be shoved, with great difficulty, and placed into empty davits.

THE LAST HOURS

One by one distant ships responded to the distress signals. The Cunard *Carpathia,* closest by, changed her course. Headed for the Mediterranean, she quickly answered the *Titanic*'s call and began to speed 58 miles (78 km) toward the sinking ship. But she was older and slower and wasn't used to going faster than about 14 to 16 knots. It would be, Captain Arthur H. Rostron estimated, almost five hours before she could get to the liner. And there was still ice to worry about and watch for.

As the *Titanic* began to sink from the front, the remaining passengers made their way to the rear of the ship, where they felt they would be safest—and farthest away from the approaching water.

And what happened to the steerage passengers? There were reports that they had been forcibly held back in their quarters. Stories were told of gates being shut, keeping these third-class passengers in their dark companionways. Some stories told of crew members keeping steerage passengers prisoner in their own quarters until most of the boats had been launched. And there are some disturbing statistics: while all the children in first

*The stern lifting above the frigid waters
of the North Atlantic, lights still ablaze,
the great ship goes down.*

and second class were saved, two-thirds of those in steerage went down with the ship. While almost all the women in first class survived the sinking, nearly half of those in third class did not.

By the time all the boats had been lowered, the ship had already begun to sink noticeably from the front. When the engineers from below finally left their posts and made their way to the top of the ship, all the lifeboats had been launched. For these brave men, it was too late. On the stern of the ship, passengers clung to whatever seemed permanent and fixed. Otherwise they would have been washed into the icy water.

The ship's orchestra, eight musicians in all, played ragtime melodies during much of the evacuation in an effort to cheer up worried passengers. Legend says they played the hymn "Nearer My God to Thee" as the ship went down, but there is some doubt about this. For one thing, this is an American hymn, and the melody would probably have been unfamiliar to English musicians. Also, every effort was made to keep people's spirits up, not to remind them that they might be about to die. The orchestra played on the promenade deck until they had to seek a drier spot, when they went up to the boat deck.

Lights continued to burn, the sea was calm, and from a distance it must have seemed as if nothing was wrong. But the line of lights blazing from the portholes and windows began to tilt as the stern of the ship rose further and further out of the water. The great ship was definitely going down.

CHAPTER FOUR

SINKING AND RESCUE

It was almost 2:20 A.M., Monday, April 15. As the angle of the ship became more and more vertical, her three propellers swung out of the water. The angle increased to 50, then 60 degrees. Even as the ship began its final plunge, few people jumped from the stern. Some witnesses insisted that the lights on board the ship stayed lit until just minutes before the vessel slid beneath the waves.

Just before that happened, a great roar went up. It was the sound of all the movable objects sliding noisily to the front of the tilting ship. Some witnesses remembered hearing the noise that one of the *Titanic*'s gigantic boilers made as it rolled from a position in the middle of the ship to the front.

Some people also recalled that the ship seemed to break in two, and that the forward part of the ship disappeared first and more quickly than the stern portion. Some eyewitnesses recalled that the funnel farthest forward toppled loose when the *Titanic* sank. Others seemed to remember that it came loose as that part of the ship met the water.

Between 12:45 and 1:45, eight white rockets had been

lighted and sent up into the sky. These are the universal signals for ships at sea when they are in trouble. There is, to this day, dispute as to whether or not a British ship named the *Californian* was near enough to have seen the rockets and answered the distress calls. But the *Californian*'s captain had already gone to bed and the wireless had been shut down for the night.

There was a strong fear that the sinking vessel would create suction when it went down. This might pull the lifeboats under with it. As a result every effort was made to get the lifeboats as far away from the ship as possible. This may be one reason why few survivors were actually rescued from the sea. Only about a dozen people found floating in the water were picked up by any of the eighteen lifeboats that had been launched from the *Titanic*. With the sea temperature around 28°F (-2°C), few could have survived very long.

THE RESCUE SHIP

Meanwhile the *Carpathia*, her engines pushed to full speed, was rushing to the scene. When she got there, at four in the morning, there was no sign of the *Titanic*. There was a floating field of wreckage and there were all the lifeboats. About 850 of the *Titanic*'s passengers had left the ship in lifeboats, and 705 of these were squeezed on board the *Carpathia*, which had been, luckily, only half full. They came aboard the *Carpathia* by whatever means was practical or possible: ladder, boatswain's chair, slings, and bags.

For four hours the *Carpathia* combed the waters near where the *Titanic* had gone down. James Bissett, the *Carpathia*'s second mate, tells this story:

Our immediate task was only too clear—to search for the people in boats or rafts, and any other survivors. The increasing daylight revealed dozens of icebergs within our horizon. Among them were four or five big bergs, towering up to two hundred feet above water level. One of these was the one that the Titanic had struck.

When the last lifeboat had come alongside the *Carpathia*, those who survived began to grasp the magnitude of the tragedy. With a sense of horror the women and children on the rescue ship began to comprehend that their husbands and fathers had gone down with the *Titanic*.

Just before the *Carpathia* began her sad voyage back to New York, Captain Rostron positioned his ship over the spot that was assumed to be where the *Titanic* had gone down. When his ship was there, he and the rescued passengers paused for a service. This memorial was to commemorate those who had lost their lives during that fateful night.

THE WORLD WAITS

Radio communication was then very new, and there was a great deal of confusion in both the United States and England about

Titanic *survivors huddled in a lifeboat alongside the* Carpathia, *waiting to be taken aboard.*

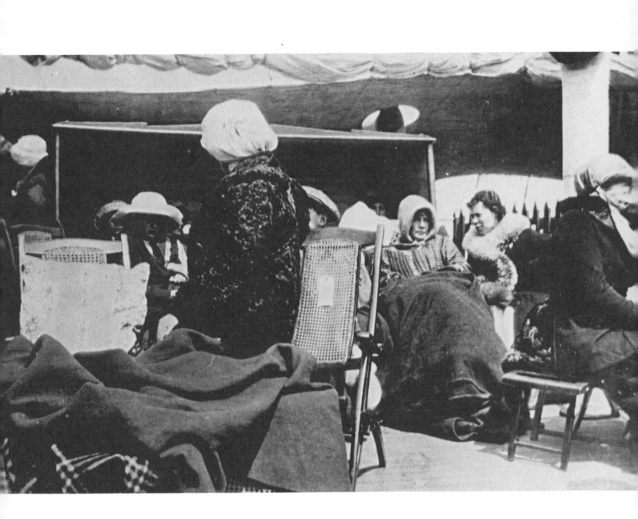

Above: *survivors of the disaster bundled in coats, scarves, and blankets on the decks of the Carpathia. Opposite: while some early reports were optimistic about the number of people who survived the disaster, the headlines in the New York Times of April 16 came very close to evaluating the loss accurately—about two-thirds of those on board the Titanic had perished.*

"All the News That's Fit to Print."

The New York Times.

THE WEATHER.

Unsettled Tuesday; Wednesday,
fair, cooler, moderate southerly
winds, becoming variable.

VOL. LXI...NO. 19,896.

NEW YORK, TUESDAY, APRIL 16, 1912.—TWENTY-FOUR PAGES.

ONE CENT In Greater New York.
TWO CENTS

TITANIC SINKS FOUR HOURS AFTER HITTING ICEBERG;
866 RESCUED BY CARPATHIA, PROBABLY 1250 PERISH;
ISMAY SAFE, MRS. ASTOR MAYBE, NOTED NAMES MISSING

Astor and Bride,
Straus and Wife,
and Maj. Butt Aboard.

"RULE OF SEA" FOLLOWED

Women and Children Put Over
in Lifeboats and Are Supposed
to be Safe on Carpathia.

PICKED UP AFTER 8 HOURS

Vincent Astor Calls at White Star
Office for News of His Father
and Leaves Weeping.

FRANKLIN HOPEFUL ALL DAY

Manager of the Line Insisted
Titanic Was Unsinkable Even
After She Had Gone Down.

HEAD OF THE LINE ABOARD

J. Bruce Ismay Making First Trip on
Gigantic Ship That Was to
Surpass All Others.

The Lost Titanic Being Towed Out of Belfast Harbor.

Biggest Liner Plunges
to the Bottom
at 2:20 A. M.

RESCUERS THERE TOO LATE

Except to Pick Up the Few Hundreds Who Took to the
Lifeboats.

WOMEN AND CHILDREN FIRST

Cunarder Carpathia Rushing
New York with the
Survivors.

SEA SEARCH FOR OTHERS

The Californian Stands By
Chance of Picking Up Other
Boats or Rafts.

OLYMPIC SENDS THE NEWS

Only Ship to Flash Wireless Messages to Shore After the
Disaster.

LATER REPORT SAVES 866.

BOSTON, April 15.—A wireless
message picked up late to-night,
relayed from the Olympic, says
that the Carpathia is on her way
to New York with 800 passengers
from the steamer Titanic aboard.
They are mostly women and children, the message said, and it concluded: "Grave fears are felt for
the safety of the balance of the
passengers and crew."

Special to The New York Times.

CAPE RACE, N. F., April 15.
—The White Star liner Olympic
reports by wireless this evening
that the Cunarder Carpathia
reached, at daybreak this morning, the position from which wireless calls for help were sent out
last night by the Titanic after the
collision with an iceberg. The
Carpathia found only the lifeboats
and the wreckage of what had
been the biggest steamship afloat.

The Titanic had foundered at
about 2:20 A. M., in latitude
41:46 north and longitude 50:14
west. This is about 30 minutes
of latitude, or about 34 miles,
south of the position at which she
struck the iceberg. All her boats
are accounted for and about 655
souls have been saved of the crew
and passengers, most of the latter
presumably women and children.

There were about 2,100 persons
aboard the Titanic.

The Leyland liner Californian is
remaining and searching the position of the disaster, while the Carpathia is returning to New York
with the survivors.

It can be positively stated that
up to 11 o'clock to-night nothing whatever had been received
at or heard by the Marconi station here to the effect that the
Parisian, Virginian or any other
ships had picked up any survivors

PARTIAL LIST OF THE SAVED.

Includes Bruce Ismay, Mrs. Widener, Mrs. H. B. Harris, and an incomplete name, suggesting
Mrs. Astor's.

Special to The New York Times.

CAPE RACE, N. F., Tuesday, April 16.—Following is a partial list of survivors among the first-
class passengers of the Titanic, received by the Marconi wireless station this morning from the Carpathia, via the steamship Olympic:

Mrs. JACOB P. ——— and maid.
Mr. HARRY ANDERSON.
Mr. ED. W. APPLETON.
Mrs. ROSE ABBOTT.
Miss G. M. BURNS.
Miss D. E. CASSEBERE.
Mr. WM. H. CLARKE.
Mrs. B. CHIBINACE.
Miss E. G. CROSSBIE.
Mr. H. ROBESIE.
Miss JEAN HIPACK.
Mrs. HY. B. HARRIS.
Mrs. ALEX. HALVERSON.
Miss MARGARET BATTS.
Mr. BRUCE ISMAY.
Mr. and Mrs. ED. KIMBERLEY.
Mr. F. A. KENNYMAN.
Mrs. EMILE KENGCHEN.
Miss G. F. LONGLEY.
Mr. A. F. LEADER.
Miss BERTHA LAVORE.
Mr. ERNEST LIVES.
Miss MARY CLINES.
Mrs. SINGRID LINDSTROM.
Mr. GUSTAVE J. LESNEUR.
Miss GEORGETTA A. MADILL.
Mrs. MELICARDI.
Miss TUCKER and maid.
Mr. J. B. THAYER.
Mr. J. B. THAYER, Jr.
Mr. HENRY WOOLNER.
Miss ANNA WARD.
Mr. RICHARD H. WILLIAMS.
Mr. F. N. WARNER.
Miss HELEN A. WILSON.
Miss WILLARD.
Miss MARY WICKS.
Mr. GEO. D. WIDENER and maid.
Mrs. J. STEWART WHITE.
Miss MARIE YOUNG.
Mr. THOMAS POTTER, Jr.
Mrs. EDNA S. ROBERTS.
Countess of ROTHES.

Mr. C. ROLMANE.
Mrs. SUSAN P. ROGERSON. (Prob-
ably two persons.)
Miss EMILY B. ROGERSON.
Mr. ARTHUR ROGERSON.
Master ALLISON and nurse.
Miss K. T. ANDREWS.
Miss NINETTE PARHART.
Mr. E. W. ALLEN.
Mr. and Mrs. D. BISHOP.
Mr. H. BLANK.
Miss A. BASSINA.
Mr. JAMES BAXTER.
Mr. GEORGE A. BATT——
Miss C BONNELL.
Mr. J. M. BROWN.
Mrs. G. C. BOWEN.
Mr. and Mrs. R. L. BECK——
Miss RUTH TAUSSIG.
Miss ELLA THOR.
Mr. and Mrs. E. Z. TAYLOR.
GILBERT M. TUCKER.
Mr. J. B. THAYER.
Mr. JOHN B. ROGERSON.
Mrs. M. ROTHSCHILD.
Miss MADELEINE NEWELL.
Mrs. MARJORIE NEWELL.
HELEN W. NEWSOM.
Mr. FIENNAD OMOND.
Mr. E. C. OSTBY.
Miss HELEN R. OSTBY.
Mrs. MAMAM J. RENAGO.
Mrs. OLIVIA.
Mrs. D. W. MERVIN.
Mr. PHILIP BROCK.
Mr. JAMES GOOGHT.
Mrs. RUBETA MAIMY.
Mr. PIERRE MARECHAL.
Mrs. W. E. MINEHAN.
Miss APPIE RANELT.
Mr. ARTUR PEUCHEN.
Mrs. EARL R. BEHR.
Miss DESSETTE.

Mrs. WILLIAM BUCKNELL.
Mrs. G. H. BARKWORTH.
Mr. H. B. STEFFASON.
Mrs. ELSIE BOWERMAN.

The Marconi station reports that
it missed the word after "Mrs. Jacob P."
In a list received by the Associated
Press this morning this name appeared
well down, but in THE TIMES list it is
first, suggesting that the name of Mrs.
John Jacob Astor is intended. This sup-
position is strengthened by the fact
that, except for Mrs. H. J. Allison—this
Mrs. Astor is the only lady in the "A" col-
umn of the ship's passenger list attended
by a maid.

NAMES PICKED UP AT BOSTON.

BOSTON, April 15.—Among the
names of survivors of the Titanic picked
up by wireless from the steamer Carpathia here to-night were the following:

Mr. and Mrs. L. HENRY.
Mrs. W. A. HOOPER.
Mr. MILE.
Mr. J. FLYNN.
Miss ALICE FORTUNE.
Mrs. ROBERT DOUGLAS.
Miss HILDA SLAYTER.
Mrs. F. SMITH.
Mr. BRAKAM.
Miss LUCILLE CARTER.
Mr. WILLIAM CARTER.
Mrs. FLORENCE MARE.
Miss ALICE PHILLIPS.
Mrs. PAULA MUNGE.
Miss PHYLLIS O.
HOWARD B. CASE.
Miss BERTHA.

It is proceeding to New York direct. We
very much fear that there has been
serious loss of life, but it is impossible
for us to say definitely concerning any
part of the situation until we are
able to reassure ourselves whether
not any of the Titanic's passengers are
aboard the Allan liners.

Special to The New York Times.

CAPT. E. J. SMITH,
Commander of the Titanic.

hours before the expected arrival of the
Virginian and the Parisian.
1,465 Lives Lost First Report.

It is unbelievable, as White Star Line
officials were compelled to concede
finally, that the Carpathia should have
failed to pick up every lifeboat which
still floated on the waves. If they
failed to pick up more than 655 passengers, it was because the others of the
ship's complement had gone with her
to the bottom.

It is to say not only nearly eight

THE PROBABLE LOSS.
Number Aboard.

First cabin	
Second cabin	
Steerage	
Crew	
Total	2,100
Saved.	
By the Carpathia	866
Probably drowned	1,250

and when Capt. Haddock's message
proved that to be untrue only the ad-
mission was made at the White Star
offices that the Titanic had sunk. Mr.
Franklin said that Capt. Haddock's
message was brief and "neglected to
say that all the crew and had been saved."

As far as we know the situation, there
have been reports from Halifax that
three steamers were at the scene of the
Titanic's sinking, namely, the Virgin-

several hundred passengers of the Titanic, is now en route to New York.
At 9 o'clock, however, he modified
this statement, declaring:

*Crowds in New York City await news about
the Titanic. Here the latest information
is being printed in large letters on a
chalkboard above the entrance to the offices
of the New York American newspaper.*

the fate of the *Titanic*. Because of garbled messages, several newspapers reported that all the passengers had been saved and the ship was being towed to Halifax, Nova Scotia. Both the *New York Evening Sun* and the *Boston Evening Transcript* made this error. *The New York Times'* information was accurate from the beginning. That paper correctly sensed the real situation and devoted its entire front page to as many of the details as were known.

In both London and New York, people who had heard rumors of the maritime disaster crowded outside the White Star offices, demanding full explanations. Although it was known within about twenty-four hours that the ship had sunk, it took almost a week to compile an accurate list of all the survivors. When the final tally was made, the list was printed in newspapers and posted in hotels, public buildings, and large stores.

When the *Carpathia* finally arrived in New York City on Thursday night, April 18, it was in a driving rainstorm. Over 30,000 curious onlookers jammed the area near the pier. It took several hours to get the survivors off the ship and to clear the pier. Then they began to give their firsthand recollections of the sinking. The same as it had been on the *Titanic,* the steerage passengers left the ship last.

One person in the crowd, however, made his way *on* to the *Carpathia*. He was Guglielmo Marconi, the inventor of the wireless. Marconi wanted to congratulate the radio operator who had been able to send messages from the *Titanic* to the *Carpathia*. It was then that Marconi met Harold Bride, who had survived the sinking. Without a doubt Marconi's invention was responsible for saving as many lives as were saved.

The legend had begun.

CHAPTER FIVE

THE INVESTIGATIONS

Just two days after the *Titanic* sank, the U.S. Senate authorized a full-scale investigation of the accident. Under Senator William Alden Smith, the examining committee was to look into the causes of the disaster. Some sense needed to be made out of what had happened during that three-hour period on April 14 and 15. An attempt was made to separate the legend from the truth, the myth from the reality.

In the American press, the British were made to look foolish. But the British got back at the Americans, when Senator Smith, in front of the Senate, made many grammatical errors and showed his lack of knowledge of the sea.

THE AMERICAN INQUIRY

It may seem strange that the United States government should be the first to set up an inquest. But many of the *Titanic*'s passengers had been wealthy Americans. And the shipping line was, for all intents and purposes, owned by a group of American financiers.

A lot of prominent Americans had gone down with the *Titanic*, and the public demanded explanations.

Over the course of several days, many passengers who survived were called on to testify. Among them was Ismay, director of the White Star Line and one of the few male passengers who survived the sinking. Several crew members also served as witnesses, including officers from the *Californian*. This was the ship that had taken so long to answer the *Titanic*'s calls for help.

No one attracted more attention than Second Officer Charles Lightoller, the highest-ranking officer on the *Titanic* to survive. Much of his testimony was extremely helpful. According to Lightoller, it was common practice to maintain speed on the North Atlantic, even with severe ice warnings. Much of what Lightoller said, and the way he presented himself, helped explain Captain Smith's interest in not slowing the vessel down. Lightoller's testimony also enhanced the White Star Line's credibility.

Under oath, Lightoller was asked at what time he had left the ship. "I didn't leave it," Lightoller replied. "Did it leave you?" asked a senator. "Yes, sir," Lightoller replied.

Several points of value were brought out during the course of the lengthy trial. The British Board of Trade was held responsible for the fact that there weren't enough lifeboats. The board's regulation stated only that a ship over 10,000 tons should carry sixteen lifeboats. The ruling made no provision for the fact that the *Titanic* was more than four times that size and would carry a great many more passengers (if not four times more) than a 10,000 ton vessel could manage. Due to this peculiar loophole, the White Star Line had acted within the law in equipping the ship. It was just that the law itself was senseless. The ship had been certified by the Board of Trade to carry as many as 3,547 people. But legally the *Titanic* was compelled to provide lifeboats for only 1,000 passengers.

Some people felt that the presence of Ismay on board had influenced Captain Smith's performance. Under this pressure Smith might have become overconfident, feeling he had to maintain the *Titanic*'s top speed. He was aware that there was ice in the region, and there should have been an order to slow the boat down. At the Senate hearings, Ismay the survivor tried to shift as much responsibility as possible onto Captain Smith—the deceased. Ironically, when the fuss about the *Titanic* was over, so was Ismay's career. A broken man, he gave up all his business ties and became a virtual recluse.

The inquest also found that the ship had not been designed carefully enough. It soon became evident that the watertight compartments were anything but watertight. The quick and careless inspection of the vessel during her sea trials was cited as another shortcoming.

Because inspection had been inadequate and lifeboat drills had not been held, the loading and lowering of the lifeboats had been a haphazard affair. It was revealed that the men on lookout in the crow's nest did not even have binoculars. If they had had

Bruce Ismay, on the right, on his way to testify at the British hearings. With him are his wife, Florence, and White Star Line General Manager Harold Sanderson.

binoculars, would they have spotted the iceberg soon enough to have missed it?

Finally the inquest raised the very serious question of the *Californian.* Where was this ship when the *Titanic* sent off its signal rockets? Had the *Californian,* as many people believed, been much closer to the troubled ship than the *Carpathia?* And wouldn't many more lives have been saved if the *Californian* had rushed to help the rapidly sinking liner instead of turning a deaf ear?

THE BRITISH VERSION

In fact, the position of the *Californian* during the *Titanic*'s last hours became a focal point of the British inquiry, which began on May 3, 1912, and continued for over a month. Almost a hundred witnesses testified during the course of the hearing.

The British investigation stressed the lessons to be learned from the tragedy. The purpose of the inquiry was to find out what had gone wrong so that it couldn't happen again. There was no interest in placing blame, especially on a captain who had given up his life with his ship.

Several crew members from the *Californian,* including that ship's captain, Stanley Lord, gave testimony early in the investigation. Since most people believed that the *Californian* had been near enough to see the rockets, the fact that that ship's log made no reference to them was suspicious. One of the worst crimes known to sailors is failure to respond to a signal for help. Although it was never conclusively proved, most observers felt that the *Californian*'s log had been altered.

The testimony of the *Californian*'s crew members showed

that their ship was "probably" no more than 5 to 10 miles (8 to 16 km) away from the *Titanic* as it lay helpless. Certainly the *Californian* was no farther than 19 miles (30 km) away and could have been on the scene before the *Titanic* sank.

Captain Rostron and his crew on the *Carpathia* came in for heavy praise, because he and his ship had done as much as was humanly possible to rescue the *Titanic*'s passengers.

Lord Mersey, head of the British Board of Trade's investigation, agreed with many of the findings of the American investigation, including those relating to crew behavior, the lowering of the lifeboats, and the fact that the ship was keeping a very fast speed in dangerous waters.

Both investigations concluded, with only minor differences in details, that the ship had been going too fast in hazardous conditions. And once the iceberg had been struck, the crew had not maintained enough order as passengers began abandoning the ship.

WHAT WAS LEARNED

The British and American investigations both identified certain changes that were needed to make the North Atlantic a safer place for all shipping. After the *Titanic*, the pay for wireless operators was increased substantially and working conditions were improved. From that time on, wireless rooms had to be staffed around the clock. The wireless operator on board the *Californian* had gone to bed shortly after the *Titanic* hit the iceberg. He never knew of the disaster until he turned his radio equipment on again in the morning. By then it was too late.

A much stricter ruling was made about the number of lifeboats available. And from that time forward steamship companies made certain there was enough lifeboat space for everyone on board all ships. Within days, several ships hastily added lifeboats to comply with these new rules. Rules for conducting serious lifeboat drills came into force. All nations joined together to make these changes. Never again would international shipping organizations allow ships with inexperienced crews to sail.

New and more demanding shipbuilding specifications were called for. Hull construction was altered so that ships' keels, or bottoms, would be stronger.

As a result of the accident, an organization called the International Ice Patrol was born. Except for the years of the two world wars, this group has been responsible ever since for alerting all shipping and for creating maps of potentially dangerous areas in the North Atlantic.

Finally, little attempt was made to rid the public of the notion that steerage passengers had been discriminated against. There was never any proof that third-class passengers had been held back forcibly on the night the *Titanic* went down. It seems they were simply ignored. And much the same indifference was exhibited during both the American and British investigations. If someone had traveled in first class, people paid attention. If they had been in steerage, no one cared.

CHAPTER SIX

THE YEARS
OF SILENCE

It is hard for us to understand the impact the disaster had on the public. The initial press coverage was enormous, and much of it was critical of the wealthy and of the ship that the wealthy had built for their use. Churchmen on both sides of the Atlantic took the rich to task and felt that those who had suffered were only getting what they deserved. A great deal of hellfire and damnation was preached against the rich and powerful.

Many survivors sold their colorful recollections of the *Titanic*'s sinking to newspapers and magazines. Often these stories were short on accuracy and long on embellishment. Tales of dastardly deeds by crew members and wealthy passengers alike circulated. Many people felt that the inspirational stories, truthful or not, were far more satisfying than the ugly tales. Thus a certain glamour, or romance, began to grow up around the hours of the sinking. For a few years following the disaster, references to the *Titanic* continued to make news and hold people's interest, but the headline-grabbing days were over.

A few days after the *Titanic*'s sinking, a small cable ship, the *Mackay-Bennett,* was sent out from Halifax, Nova Scotia. Its sad task was to recover as many bodies as possible from the area where the liner sank. The ship spent two weeks searching and eventually found just over 300 bodies. The ship brought 190 of those bodies back to shore for burial. One of them was John Jacob Astor. The rest were buried at sea.

Survivors and families of those who had perished sued the White Star Line for vast sums of money. But most of the claims were settled privately and for reduced amounts. These suits dragged on until 1916, when they were finally cleared up. For the record, the White Star Line paid a total of only $665,000 in damages. This is a strikingly low figure in light of the original claims totaling some $16 million to $18 million.

Insurance claims covered the loss of most of the ship's cargo, which wasn't particularly rich or remarkable anyway. A value of $420,000 was placed on the contents of the ship's hold. The cargo seemed to be made up of some very ordinary things: sponges, wine, and oak beams, among other items. Other freight included cases of orchids, crates of shelled walnuts, and 900 rolls of linoleum!

One of the single most valuable items was a rare edition of *The Rubaiyat of Omar Khayyam.* This particular copy had a binding encrusted with over a thousand jewels. Stories were told of one passenger who had an $11,000 diamond necklace. A Philadelphia banker had placed gold coins and bullion worth $50,000 in the ship's safe.

For almost forty years very little was heard about the *Titanic.* From 1915 to 1955 no books were published about the collision. Then in 1955 Walter Lord wrote his account of the sinking, *A*

Night to Remember, which re-creates the exciting tale of the *Titanic*'s first and last voyage. For a whole new generation of readers the story took on new importance.

LARGER AND FASTER SHIPS

In the years following the sinking the name *Titanic* came to stand for any kind of major disaster, and the expression "just the tip of the iceberg" suggested that something had hidden dangers. But horrible as the accident had been, it did not stop anyone from building bigger, faster, and grander ships. Around the corner were the *Berengaria,* the *Leviathan,* and the *Majestic.* The late twenties ushered in the dazzling streamlined German ships, the *Europa* and the *Bremen.* Superliners reached their peak in the middle thirties. Both the *Normandie* and *Queen Mary* arrived on the scene in the years just before World War II. Even then liners were still the only way to go!

The White Star Line tried to forget the *Titanic,* but it couldn't. The company had planned a third liner to run on the express route between Southampton and New York along with the *Titanic* and the *Olympic.* This ship, the *Britannic,* was launched in 1914, but because of World War I she never saw commercial service. The *Britannic* served as a hospital ship during the war and was destroyed by the enemy in 1916 off the coast of Greece.

Almost immediately after the *Titanic* sank, the *Olympic* had her bulkheads strengthened and the number of lifeboats was increased. She sailed quietly and safely, a popular ship, until she was retired in the early 1930s, a victim of old age and the Depression. But the White Star Line was never quite the same, and eventually merged with its rival, Cunard. The Cunard White Star

Line was formed, and lasted for a while, but by the end of the 1940s the "White Star" part of the name was absorbed. Cunard Line became the company name, and White Star was gone forever.

Walter Lord's book generated new interest in the ship. Over a hundred books were published and a dozen movies were released in which the *Titanic* was featured. In 1960 a scene in the Broadway musical *The Unsinkable Molly Brown* showed the legendary and eccentric Molly Brown in charge of one of the ship's lifeboats.

In 1963 interested fans joined together to form an organization. By 1974 the group had become strong and large enough to call themselves the Titanic Historical Society, Inc.

As the years went on, more and more of the survivors grew old and many of them died. Each year means fewer and fewer survivors. Even someone who was on the *Titanic* as a small child would now be close to eighty.

RENEWED INTEREST

As the sixties turned into the seventies, people began to realize that science and technology had made enormous strides. Adventurers began to dream of raising the *Titanic* even though it

A scene from the Twentieth Century-Fox movie Titanic, *made in 1953*

was probably under 2.5 miles (4 km) of water in the North Atlantic, somewhere off the Grand Banks of Newfoundland.

Some people dreamed of remarkable schemes to raise the ship. Some of the ideas had possibilities and some were preposterous. And even if the ideas were good ones, the cost would be incredible. Very few people or organizations could find the money to raise the ship. And before the *Titanic* could be raised, the ship had to be found.

One of the people who was fascinated by the story of the *Titanic* was an Englishman named Douglas Woolley. In the 1960s he devised several schemes for raising the ship. Later, he claimed to have acquired the rights and ownership of the wreck. He managed to get the attention of the news media, but he had a much harder time finding the enormous sums of money it was going to take to make any of his ideas become a reality. And so nothing came of his ideas. But people listened to what he was saying, and they became more and more interested in the possibilities of going down and raising the ship.

A Welshman, John Pierce, planned to raise the hull by attaching canvas bags to it. Hydrogen would then be pumped into the bags and the ship would rise. As recently as 1979 Pierce wanted to wrap the liner in a net. After that he would pump nitrogen into the net. Then the nitrogen would freeze and, like ice cubes in a drink, the ship would float to the surface.

Another person planned to inject ping-pong balls into the ship's hull through a long pipe or hose. Then the ship would float and rise to the top. But no one seemed able to raise the money such an operation would take.

And then in the early 1980s several people came very close to finding the sunken ship. A wealthy Texas businessman named

Jack Grimm spent $2 million on three separate missions that failed to locate the *Titanic*. By donating money for equipment, he got the support of two important research organizations: Lamont-Doherty Geological Observatory and Scripps Institution of Oceanography. At one point in 1981 Grimm and his team on board the research vessel *Gyre* thought they had sighted one of the ship's three propellers. And Grimm's team from Columbia University spent part of the summer of 1983 searching, but they ran out of money.

Many people had given up hope that the great ship would ever be found.

CHAPTER SEVEN

THE GREAT SHIP
IS FOUND

But then something exciting happened. A group of scientists who were testing underwater video equipment on board the oceanographic research vessel *Knorr* were just about to finish their day's work. They had, after all, spent several weeks in search of the *Titanic* and were getting bored with the routine of their task. Suddenly an object that struck them as familiar flashed across their TV monitors.

Someone ventured out loud that it looked like one of the *Titanic*'s huge boilers. It was an image they had studied from old photographs provided by the ship's builders. It was shortly after 1:00 A.M. on September 1, 1985. Everything began to fall into place. The *Titanic,* or at least some portion of it, had been found.

Suddenly, after almost seventy-five years, the *Titanic* made newspaper headlines all over again.

The *Titanic* was pretty much where everyone thought she would be, 500 miles (800 km) south of Newfoundland. The precise resting place of the ship had always been a little uncertain. The original coordinates had been given as 41 degrees 46 minutes

North and 50 degrees 14 minutes West. But no one could ever be sure. Even the slightest deviation from these bearings could mean a variation of many square miles. And there was always the chance that the ship had drifted from this assumed position on its way 2.5 miles (4 km) down to the bottom.

It was the computerized instrument *Argo* that had actually sighted the ship. The size of a small car, the *Argo* weighs 4,000 pounds (1,800 kg). It is attached to the "mother" ship by a thick cable. The vehicle is towed through the ocean, like a sled, from 50 to 100 feet (15 to 30 m) above the ocean bottom. The *Argo* is armed with powerful cameras and strobe lights to light the ocean, which is pitch dark at that depth. There it can take video pictures of objects hidden from normal view and relay them to the surface.

What the *Argo* found was the *Titanic*'s final resting place. The ship was discovered sitting upright but appeared to be in sections. The stern, or rear, section of the ship was about 2,600 feet (800 m) away from the rest of the ship. It seems that the middle portion—covering a length of about 300 feet (90 m)—is still unaccounted for. It may have broken up on the way down and then disintegrated.

All four of the majestic funnels were missing. At one point the *Argo* bumped into part of the ship's superstructure. When the instrument resurfaced there was a smudge of black paint on its surface.

Once the ship was found, another vehicle was pressed into service. Over a period of five days, ANGUS, an even smaller instrument, made three trips to the site. Also towed along like a sled attached to the support ship, ANGUS took color photographs. During these trips, both ANGUS and the *Argo* took more than twelve thousand photographs, many of which would appear in newspapers and magazines as news of the ship's discovery became known.

The discovery of the *Titanic* was due in large part to the persistence of Robert D. Ballard, a marine geologist from the Woods Hole Oceanographic Institution, and head of the institution's Deep Submergence Laboratory. An untiring worker, Ballard became interested in the *Titanic* through a friend. Using his skills as a scientist and engineer he helped to develop the *Argo,* primarily for searching for underwater objects.

Ballard and his team of scientists, and a group of French oceanographers from the Research Institute for the Exploration of the Sea (IFREMER), had spent several weeks narrowing the position of the Titanic down from 150 square miles (390 sq km) to 30 square miles (80 sq km). At that point the *Argo* could be used to locate the wreck visually.

In 1985 there was intense excitement over the discovery and the photographing of the lost wreck after all the years of mystery. There was enthusiasm that the ship seemed to be so well preserved, even though it was in pieces. In the "debris field" be-

Above: *one of the first photographs released in 1985 of the* Titanic's *remains was of the ship's bow, with anchor chains, winches, and capstans (vertical cylinders) clearly visible.* Below: *a copper pot, in very good condition, rests on the ocean floor.*

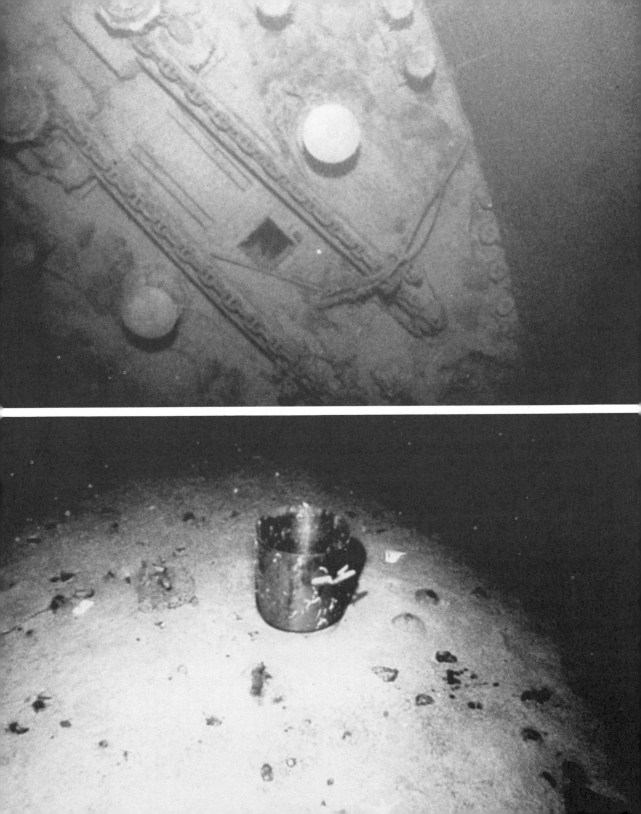

tween the front and rear portions of the ship, photographs were taken of bedsprings, silver serving trays and ice buckets, chamber pots, and suitcases. All the objects were lying on the ocean floor, and many of them seemed to be in pristine condition.

NEW QUESTIONS ASKED

Within a month of the discovery Ballard appeared before Congress to request that the *Titanic* be made an International Memorial. This designation would keep the wreck safe from treasure hunters and looters, even though the expense of getting down to the ship would be prohibitive for most people.

But was there any treasure to be found? Some people estimated that the gold and silver left on the ship would fetch hundreds of millions of dollars. But that is mostly speculation. No one really knows for sure. The cargo manifest itself shows few riches. And while some of the ship is in first-rate condition, other parts of it seem to be completely ruined.

Nobody is quite sure who owns what is left of the *Titanic*. In 1985 a British court ruled that Britain had no claims to a wreck in international waters. And all the insurance claims have long since been settled. A British company, Commercial Union, may have some legal claim to the ship's contents. They were not the original insurers but are the successors to the company that handled the original claims. Cunard Line, which eventually came to own the White Star Line, does not feel that it owns the ship.

The discovery of the *Titanic* started people thinking once more about the future of the vessel. Some people feel that the ship ought to be left as it was found, as a memorial to the people who lost their lives in 1912. And others want to bring some of the artifacts to the surface for history's sake. In many ways it appears that there is a very thin line that distinguishes underwater treasure hunters from those who believe in preserving the past for its own sake.

Shortly after the September 1 discovery of the *Titanic* a group of people stood on the stern of the *Knorr*. They were on the surface just about over the spot where the great ship had gone down. It was late at night, almost at the same hour that seventy-three years earlier the *Titanic* had begun to lose its struggle against the rushing Atlantic waters. The group held a memorial service for those lost in the disaster.

CHAPTER EIGHT

THE STORY CONTINUES

Almost as soon as the 1985 dives were over, Ballard and his team began to make plans for a return visit in 1986. Although he wanted to leave the vessel as it had been found, Ballard was determined to be on board a manned submersible that would descend the next summer and get close to the wreck.

And that is exactly what happened. During eleven days in July 1986, Ballard and his team went down to photograph the *Titanic* even more closely than they had the summer before.

This time they were aided by the *Alvin,* a twenty-year-old submersible capable of holding three people. Initially designed to descend to about 6,000 feet (1,800 m), the vessel had been completely reinforced so that she could go down comfortably to 13,000 feet (3,900 m).

It took the fifty-six researchers four days to sail the research vessel *Atlantis II* from Woods Hole Oceanographic Institution in Massachusetts to the *Titanic* site. Each day followed a similar pattern: the *Alvin* would begin its two-and-a-half-hour descent

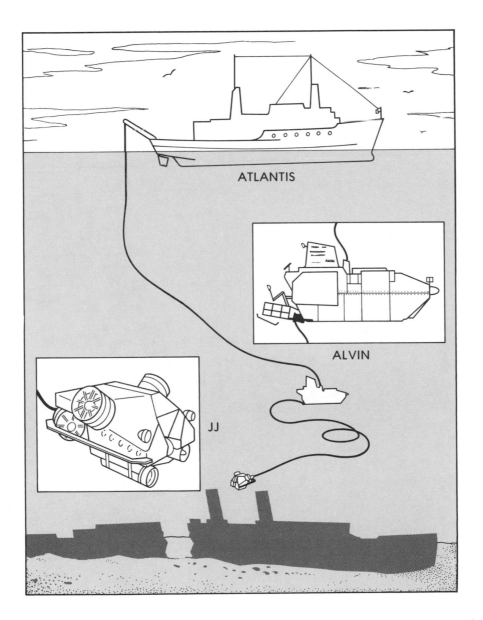

ATLANTIS

ALVIN

JJ

The research vessel Atlantis II *and
its manned submersible* Alvin

to the *Titanic* shortly after breakfast. It spent about four hours of the day at the bottom, followed by the two-and-a-half-hour ascent back to the *Atlantis II*. Attached to the *Alvin* by a tether was a new remotely operated instrument: Jason Junior, also known as JJ.

On the third day this camera-equipped robot actually entered the liner's interior. There, in the great liner's grand ballroom, JJ took the now famous photographs of one of the ship's crystal light fixtures. JJ was the first "visitor" to the ship since April of 1912.

A deep-diving robot developed for the U.S. Navy, JJ is about the size of a lawn mower. It weighs about 250 pounds (113 kg) and was attached to the *Alvin* by a 250-foot-long (75 m) electric cable. Martin Bowen piloted JJ by remote control. The 20-inch-high (50 cm) by 24-inch-wide (60 cm) apparatus is small enough to fit into places where none of the previous instruments could go. It takes high-resolution color photos and video pictures. On the 1986 mission the video images were then transmitted back to the three crew members inside the *Alvin*.

JJ's photographs helped to clear up more elements of the mystery. The grand staircase was there, minus the wood. All non-metal objects seemed to have disappeared, eaten away by marine organisms over the years. But most of the metal remains well preserved. Ballard discovered, however, that much of the iron hull plating is covered with what he describes as "rustsicles."

JJ's pictures also made clear where the ship had split apart: just in front of the third funnel. Even more objects were found in 1986 on the ocean floor in the space between the two parts of the ship: a doll's head, shoes, and four of the ship's safes. The *Alvin's* robot arm tried to open one of the safes, but nothing would

Right: a sea pen, a feather-shaped marine organism, makes its home in one of the Titanic's crystal light fixtures. This somewhat blurred black and white photo was converted from colored video film shot by JJ. Below: the elongated shapes of "rustsicles" cover one of the portholes.

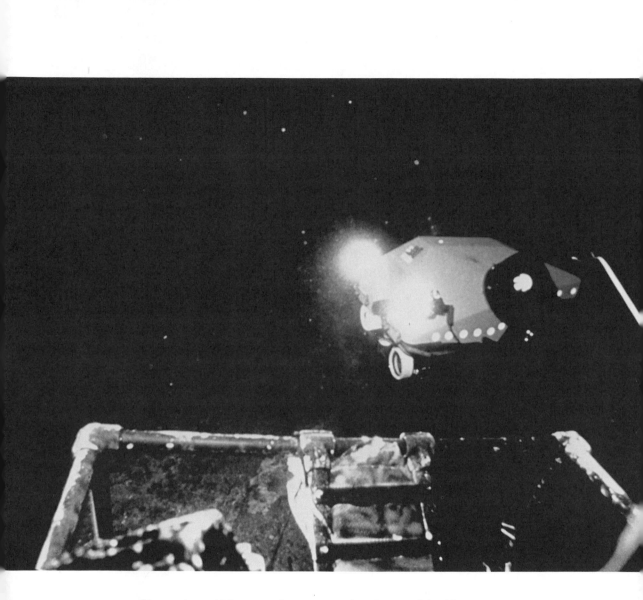

The robot JJ leaves the manned submersible Alvin
and sets out for a day's work photographing
the remains of the Titanic, some 13,000 feet
(3,900 m) below the surface of the North Atlantic.

budge the rusted door. By and large the objects strewn on the ocean floor were those belonging to steerage passengers, not first- or second-class ones.

NEW EVIDENCE

Eleven days, sixty hours and over sixty thousand still photos later, JJ had completed its task. Some other things became clearer in the 1986 photos. It was determined that the stern section had swiveled 180 degrees after breaking away at or near the surface. The remains of the stern section are heavily damaged and have many sharp parts that make exploration, even by a robot, hazardous. There is always the worry that the tether line would get caught.

The most significant finding of all was that there is no sign of the 300-foot-long (90 m) gash that had always been accepted as the reason the *Titanic* sank. What Ballard found instead was evidence of buckled and torn plates of the metal sheathing on the ship's hull. This damage must have occurred when the *Titanic* struck the iceberg.

The bow is now buried in 50 feet (15 m) of silt and mud, almost up to the anchors. Just at the point where the ship broke apart, Ballard was able to see the buckled plates and sheared rivets below the waterline. These "tears" were near the fins that had been designed to minimize rolling of the vessel. They would have been enough to send the ship to the bottom. It is also possible, however, that some of these plates were torn when the ship actually hit the ocean bottom.

Most people are now convinced that the *Titanic*'s split and broken hull could not and should not be salvaged. Ballard feels it would be impossible since the bow is broken in several places.

But Jack Grimm is determined to go diving for artifacts to bring back. He is the first to admit, however, that very exceptional and expensive diving would be required.

Running the *Alvin* is an expensive proposition. It costs about $20,000 a day to operate the submersible and "mother" ship. The total cost of operating JJ for the twelve days was $220,000 and this was funded by the U.S. Navy. The *Alvin*'s crew can stay down only a few hours before the limited battery supply of oxygen is used up. The *Alvin* is also very slow, going only at about 1 mile (1.6 km) an hour. Any other available submersibles would be just as costly. So there may be no further trips down to the *Titanic*.

As a result of the 1985 and 1986 dives, Ballard and his researchers hope to put together a "mosaic" picture, joining together photographs of small sections of the *Titanic* to make a recognizable whole. In this way the liner can be studied more carefully and perhaps even more can be learned about exactly why and how she went down.

On the *Alvin*'s seventh dive, Ballard and his team placed a memorial plaque donated by the Titanic Historical Society on the sunken vessel. The stern was the last part of the ship to remain afloat. It was also the place where the largest number of people died, so that is where they left it. The inscription on it reads, in part:

IN MEMORY OF THOSE
SOULS WHO PERISHED
WITH THE *TITANIC*,
APRIL 14–15, 1912.

The sentiment speaks for many people who believe that we have learned all that the *Titanic* can teach us.

And there is a very real question whether or not anything more can even be done. The ship has been found. Even if the money were available, could the *Titanic* be raised without everything falling to pieces? And if it could be raised, what would anybody want with a broken up luxury liner?

Seventy-five years ago there were hundreds of ships of all kinds and sizes sailing between England and the United States. Today there is only one luxury liner crossing the Atlantic from New York on a regular basis. Only the *Queen Elizabeth 2* sails on the North Atlantic route, and then only occasionally. The only people who go to Europe by boat these days are either terrified of flying or can afford to spend a week in the hotel-like luxury of the *Queen Elizabeth 2*. The superliner is almost as extinct as the dinosaur.

It seems incredible that, as late as 1985, after the discovery of the broken liner, a Welshman named John Pierce wanted to raise and restore the liner to the Southampton-New York run! And how many people would want to travel on a ship called the *Titanic*?

TITANIC TRIVIA

The British and American inquiries produced over 2,000 pages of testimony for future research and interest.

There were thirteen couples on board who were celebrating their honeymoons.

Three million rivets were used to fasten the ship together.

The ship had three anchors in the bow, one on each side, and one on top of the bow at the front. Together these anchors weighed 31 tons.

The rudder at the back that steered the ship weighed just over 100 tons.

There were thirty-one maids, valets, and governesses aboard. This meant that every fourth or fifth family was attended by some kind of servant.

There were 35,000 eggs on board the *Titanic* on her crossing. These were intended for use on the ship, to be eaten by the passengers and crew.

In order to serve meals to passengers in all three classes, there were about 12,000 dinner plates.

First-class bathtubs had hot and cold running water—both fresh water *and* salt water.

It probably took the ship about fifteen minutes to sink to her resting place on the ocean bottom. This meant she was descending at roughly 10 miles (16 km) per hour.

None of the officers who survived the *Titanic* sinking was ever given his own command.

One of the rumors that has surrounded the ship's sinking was that Captain Smith committed suicide shortly before the ship sank. There were also repeated, but unconfirmed, stories that he had survived and spent the rest of his days wandering around the Great Lakes region! No one seemed to ask why Captain Smith, an Englishman, would choose the United States for his final days.

As soon as the ship sank, rumors began to circulate that a replacement ship would be built. Her name? *Gigantic.*

GLOSSARY

Boat deck. A deck on a ship, usually above the promenade deck. On the *Titanic,* it was the deck where the lifeboats were stowed.

Bow. The front, pointed end of a ship.

Crow's nest. An open receptacle halfway up the forward mast that could hold (usually) two people who served as lookouts.

Davit. A vertical metal support, to which a ship's lifeboat is attached at either end.

Flagship. The most important vessel of a shipping company, and usually the largest ship.

Keel. The bottommost part of a ship, running from bow to stern.

Knot. One nautical mile, or 6,076 feet (1,852 m), per hour. It is slightly longer than a land mile. A knot is the traditional way that a ship's speed, in hours, is expressed.

Mast. Most steamships of the early twentieth century carried a mast at the front of the ship and one at the rear. They were holdovers from the days of sailing ships, when several masts were necessary to handle the sail riggings. By the time of the

Titanic they were still used for some wiring and rigging, but their existence was primarily for the sake of appearance.

Port. If you are standing on a ship and facing the front, the left hand side of the ship is called the port side.

Promenade deck. One of the main decks of a ship. On the *Titanic,* the deck was glass enclosed for easy walking in all kinds of weather. Most of the first-class public rooms were on this deck.

Propeller. Also known as a screw (because of the scientific principle upon which it works). The *Titanic* had three propellers that drove the ship. She was, therefore, referred to as a "triple-screw" ship.

Rudder. A large, flat piece of metal under the stern of a ship that is used for steering.

Sister ship. A second ship that is similar, but not always identical, to another ship. The *Olympic* and *Titanic* were sister ships and looked very much alike. But the *Titanic* measured about a thousand tons more and there were subtle differences between them.

Starboard. If you are standing on a ship and facing the front, the right hand side of the ship is called the starboard side. Another way to remember: the letter R (for right) is directly next to the letter S (for starboard) in the alphabet.

Stern. The rear of a ship is known as the stern.

Waterline. The bottom of the *Titanic* was painted red, and the sides of the ship were black. The division, where those lines met, was the waterline, and indicated how the ship should "ride" in the water.

FOR FURTHER READING

BOOKS

Baldwin, Hanson W. *Sea Fights and Shipwrecks*. Garden City, N.Y.: Hanover House, 1938, 1955.

Brinnin, John Malcolm. *The Sway of the Grand Saloon: A Social History of the North Atlantic*. New York: Delacorte Press, 1971.

Hoehling, A.A. *Great Ship Disasters*. Chicago: Cowles Book Co. (Henry Regnery), 1971.

Hoffman, William, and Grimm, Jack. *Beyond Reach: The Search for the Titanic*. New York and Toronto: Beaufort Books, 1982.

Lord, Walter. *A Night to Remember*. New York: Holt, Rinehart and Winston, 1955.

Lord, Walter. *The Night Lives On*. New York: William Morrow and Co., 1986.

Marcus, Geoffrey. *The Maiden Voyage*. New York: Viking Press, 1969.

Rosenbaum, Robert A., ed. *Best Book of True Ship Stories*. New York: Doubleday, 1966. This is particularly interesting as the book includes a firsthand recollection by Sir James Bissett. He was second mate aboard the *Carpathia* the day it rescued so many of the *Titanic*'s passengers. Bissett went on to distinguish himself and later became captain of both the *Queen Mary* and the *Queen Elizabeth*.

Shaw, Frank H. *Full Fathom Five, A Book of Famous Shipwrecks.* New York: Macmillan, 1930.

Wall, Robert. *Ocean Liners.* New York: E. P. Dutton, 1977.

MONOGRAPHS

There are an amazing number of articles and pamphlets on the *Titanic*. Many of them are reprints of firsthand accounts of the sinking by officers and passengers who survived. They make fascinating if not always reliable reading.

Dodge, Washington. *The Loss of the Titanic.* Riverside, Conn: 7C's Press. Originally an address delivered by the author to the Commonwealth Club, San Francisco. May 11, 1912.

Lightoller, Charles. *Titanic.* Riverside, Conn.: 7C's Press (first published in 1935, revised in 1975).

Thayer, John B. *The Sinking of the S.S. Titanic.* Riverside, Conn: 7C's Press, 1974 (first published in 1940).

Watson, Arnold and Betty. *Roster of Valor, The Titanic Halifax Legacy.* Riverside, Conn: 7C's Press, 1984.

The Deathless Story of the Titanic. Riverside, Conn.: 7C's Press.

The Sinking of the Titanic and Great Sea Disasters. Philadelphia: International Bible House. In this original edition, the copyright is 1912. The introduction is a "spiritual consolation" by Henry Van Dyke, and it is dated April 18, 1912—just three days after the *Titanic* sank.

MAGAZINES, ETC.

Almost the only way to get information about the 1985 and 1986 dives to the ship is from newspapers and news magazines that covered the events. *Science News, Time, Newsweek,* and *U.S. News and World Report* have all given a fair amount of coverage to the two years of undersea exploration. *Popular Mechanics,* in its December 1985 issue, shows a lot of ways for raising the ship. Both *National Geographic* and *Smithsonian* have more reflective pieces. A quarterly publication by Woods Hole Oceanographic Institution, *Oceanus* (vol. 28, no. 4, winter 1985/86), not only covers the 1985 dive but reviews a great deal of the past history with plenty of documentary illustrations. The 1986 expedition is documented in the December issue of *National Geographic;* in *Oceanus* (vol. 29, no. 3, fall 1986); and in the National Geographic video entitled *Secrets of the Titanic,* released by Vestron/Inovision, Stamford, Conn.

INDEX

ABOUT THE AUTHOR

Frank Sloan has been part of the world of children's books for many years—in production, art direction, editing, and now, with the writing of *Titanic*, he takes his place among the authors of nonfiction for young people.

A long-time *Titanic* buff, Mr. Sloan has over the years followed with fascination the efforts of various entrepreneurs and adventurers to find the long-lost ship and recover its rumored treasures. When a joint American-French scientific expedition found the wreck off the coast of Newfoundland in 1985, he knew that it was time to retell the story of this great ship and its tragic end.

Frank Sloan is senior editor at Franklin Watts and makes his home in New York City.